"With genuine spiritual and intellectual genius, Stephen Doetsu Snyder explores a revered Buddhist text in modern, radically liberating ways. I was jolted on every page with heart-opening joy at the good news of our true nature: the original nature of all things right under our noses, endlessly renewed by its mysterious source. This is a magnificent, breakthrough book that will be accessible and helpful to anyone at any point on their path."

—Rick Hanson, PhD, *New York Times* best-selling author of *Neurodharma* and *Buddha's Brain*

"With refreshing directness and clarity, Stephen Doetsu Snyder unpacks the teachings contained in the 'Trust in Awakening' poem, showing that awakening is accessible to all of us. One of those no-frills books that shows that all good teachings are simple in presentation, yet profound in scope."

—Vanessa Zuisei Goddard, Zen teacher, author of *Still Running*

"In this book, Stephen Doetsu Snyder has produced a fresh and unusually open translation of the 'Xin Xin Ming,' one of Zen's most poetic teachings of nonduality. He presents brief, easily understood, and poignant commentaries on each verse that constitute direct pointing out instructions for awakening. Students of Buddhadharma will find this book a fresh, modern perspective on an ancient classic."

—Diane Musho Hamilton, Soto Zen teacher and author of *Compassionate Conversations*

"Stephen Doetsu Snyder's long trainings in both Theravada and Zen practice mean that he is able to offer a very valuable perspective on this great Zen poem, often considered to be the first and still one of the greatest presentations of the discoveries of our fundamental nature that Zen/Chan has been opening up for practitioners throughout its long history."

—Henry Shukman, author of *One Blade of Grass* and spiritual director of Mountain Cloud Zen Center

"Stephen Doetsu Snyder's beautiful commentary on the ancient poem 'Faith in Mind' speaks with unusual clarity about the experience of meeting true reality. Snyder's description of such experiences are inspiring to the beginning meditator and confirming to the experienced meditator. His book is a valuable addition to the literature on this subject."

—Roshi Joan Hogetsu Hoeberichts, Abbot of Heart Circle Zen

"A truly unique book that speaks to the many facets of the spiritual path with potent authenticity. Snyder's beautiful quatrains vibrate with direct transmission, and his skillful commentary effortlessly unfolds layers of meaning. This is a book of rare richness and clarity and is sure to be cherished by all who read it."

—Steve James, educator, founder of the Movement Koan Method, and host of the *Guru Viking* podcast

"Stephen Doetsu Snyder draws on his own clear seeing to help us access greater freedom by experiencing our true identity. Snyder has a unique capacity to use language to transmit that which extends further and deeper than words but is always vibrantly alive and evolving within and around us. We are graced with the opportunity to invite his rendering of the 'Xin Xin Ming' and his commentary to land directly in our awareness so that we may be opened to, and trust in, our own awakening."

—Marisa Mohrer, LMSW, MPH, trauma therapist and author of *Songs of Awakening*

"A wonderful and beautifully written book, based on the fascinating 'Xin Xin Ming' poem, where Stephen Doetsu Snyder describes the unconditioned reality from his own direct experience! With poetic and clear language, readers are invited to explore and align their mind with the source of all reality."

—Thomas Jedensjö, Buddhist practitioner, Sweden

"Rooted in—but not limited by—tradition, Stephen Snyder's authentic realization refreshes and enlivens us according to our capacity, increasing our ability to trust and persevere on the way. *Trust in Awakening* begins with one of the most revered poems in the long history of Cha'n Zen, and points directly to the heart of the matter, with refreshing conviction and trademark sincerity. I can't recommend this work more sincerely."

—Felicia Eiki Horne, LCSW, retired psychotherapist, award-winning storyteller and playwright

TRUST IN AWAKENING

TRUST
in
AWAKENING

A Zen Teaching on
Accessing the Absolute

STEPHEN SNYDER

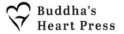
Buddha's
Heart Press

Buddha's Heart Press
awakeningdharma.org
Midland, MI, USA

Library of Congress Control Number: 2022914980
ISBN: 978-1-7347810-7-6 (paperback)
ISBN: 978-1-7347810-8-3 (e-book)

Editing by Lynn Slobogian
Proofreading by Eva van Emden
Illustrations by Samuel Quinn
Cover and interior design by Jazmin Welch (fleck creative studio)
Cover photography by Praniket Desai via Unsplash
E-book production by Legible Publishing Services
Project management by Carra Simpson

For my teacher Mark Sando Mininberg Roshi and his teachers Bernie Tetsugen Glassman Roshi and John Daido Loori Roshi—with gratitude for their inspiration, abiding love, and dedication to the dharma and supporting realization in their students.

contents

FOREWORD xi

PREFACE xv

TRUST IN AWAKENING 1

COMMENTARY 45

GLOSSARY 85

Foreword

I was first introduced to Stephen Snyder through his book *Practicing the Jhānas*, an in-depth presentation of traditional Theravada Buddhist meditation. Stephen was one of the first Westerners to master these teachings and receive recognition of his attainments by being authorized as a Theravada teacher from Pa Auk Sayadaw, one of Buddhism's great meditation masters. Stephen also trained for many years in the Zen (Ch'an) school and is a recognized teacher in that tradition as well. Seeking to deepen my own Zen practice, I came across a copy of his groundbreaking *Demystifying Awakening*, a presentation of the spiritual path that brings together, perhaps for the first time, the best of Theravada and Zen teaching into one system. Inspired, I reached out to Stephen in hopes of studying the *jhānas* and associated heart practices with him. Little did I know how transformative my encounter with Stephen and his teaching would come to be.

In this newest book, Stephen brings his unique and powerful teaching to the *Xin Xin Ming*, known in the West as the *Faith in Mind* poem, traditionally attributed to the Third Zen Patriarch Sengcan (529–613 AD). This deeply revered poem is both a profound statement on the nature of reality and a teaching that has guided Zen students to Awakening for the last 1,500 years. In Zen, the word "mind" does not refer to our brain or our thoughts or even our ordinary individual consciousness, with all its prejudices and limitations. Instead, the poem is pointing us to awaken to a mind that is free of grasping and open to the joy of all experience, in this very moment. This mind is our true nature awaiting silently to welcome each one of us, if only we can drop our resistances and see that we're already home.

Stephen's method in this case is to provide us with a clarification of both our ordinary conception of self-identity and the awakened or realized view of the Absolute as identity. His rendering of the poem and his commentary provides what is known in the Zen tradition as a direct pointing to the mind, outside words and letters. That is, providing us the opportunity to quietly contemplate each line and allow its deeper meaning to arise and help awaken us to our own true nature. Every two lines bear a relationship either confirming a view or revealing a contrast. Each stanza of four lines can be contemplated together. This authentic Zen practice, offered by one of our finest living spiritual teachers, is a gift to anyone willing to enter and experience its depth and potential for Awakening.

For my part, I can attest that Stephen's teaching, arising from his own dedicated practice, is transformative for students at any level of experience. Trust that you are in the hands of a sincere and compassionate meditation master and dive deep into your own Awakening.

Mark Sando Mininberg
ROSHI

Preface

The *Xin Xin Ming* is considered the first poem of Zen (Ch'an). It is far more than simply a poem. It is a direct pointing to the source—the Absolute—and the Absolute in each of us that we call "true nature." It is considered a direct teaching in Zen. A direct teaching is presented with as little conceptual framing as possible. It is pointing to the source itself again and again in different voices. A direct teaching cuts through theorizing and lands us directly in the Absolute or in one of its functions—Absence (emptiness) or Presence being core functions. (Please see the glossary for definitions of new or unfamiliar terms.)

During my nearly fifty years of Zen practice I have turned to this poem as a source of inspiration, a map of sorts to the path of no path. This poem gives subtle pointers, then removes the concepts from those pointers, leaving the direct knowing of truth.

I wrote this book to be a companion to my books *Buddha's Heart* (describing the ancient Buddhist heart practices) and *Demystifying Awakening* (revealing the process, impact, and path of Awakening). I want this book to be a nonconceptual vehicle of direct pointing to the source, the truth, the inherent nature of us all.

While this book can be used at any stage of spiritual development or realization, it is most beneficial in the hands of one who feels the burn for Awakening, that all-consuming fire drawing one toward deeper and deeper absolute truth. This book can be the catalyst for that explosion of Awakening we call *kenshō* in Zen. *Kenshō* is seeing your true nature—that is, seeing the Absolute, the source, fully manifesting as you.

May this book spark your Awakening!

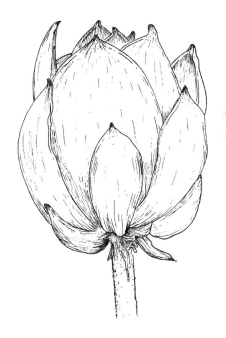

TRUST IN AWAKENING

I.

The Great Way is effortless

With no preferences

Surrender desire and aversion

Clarity dazzles

II.

Any distinction

The distance between heaven and earth

Awakening *nibbāna*

Acquits for or against

III.

Clutch likes and dislikes

The principal mind disease

Not consummating true nature

Agitates the mind

IV.

Vast, boundless space

Perfect Absence

Preserve preferences

Cloak the wisdom eye

V.

Refrain from living in the world

Refrain from pursuing Absence

Repose in harmonious love

Polarities gone

VI.

Not traversing the pathway

Judgments bewilder

Regard the worldly as authentic

Obscure reality

VII.

Refuse the worldly

Veil the Absolute

Propagate thought and concept

Elude truth

VIII.

Unbind thought and concept

Roam openly

Inhabit the source

Know all meaning

IX.

Awakening dawns

Eclipse form and Absence

No beginning, no end

Sever every opinion

X.

Abiding in Absence

Conceit humbles

Residing in wisdom

Quiet confidence

XI.

Ceaseless freedom

Abiding in clarity

Unmanifest and manifest Absolute

Immaculate non-doing

XII.

Move freely

Eternal now

No locus of awareness

Suchness unfolds

XIII.

Kalāpa universe

Dissolving boundaries

Universe *kalāpa*

Openly unconditioned

XIV.

Being is non-being

Absence

Non-being is being

Manifestation

XV.

Diamondlike clarity

Vison penetrates

Absence is form

Form is Absence

XVI.

Awake

Who is holy or wise

Uninhibited trust

Heartful modesty

XVII.

Heavenly contentment

Without past or future

Without here or there

Trust in Awakening

Commentary

I.

THE GREAT WAY IS EFFORTLESS

The Great Way is the path of spiritual development and the unfolding of Awakening. "Being effortless" means no doer or sense of self is taking action. When we bring effort to an activity, we bring our thoughts and conceptual understanding to it. But neither thought nor concepts abide in the Absolute. When we understand how to dismiss the sense of self from effort, our action becomes effortless and we begin walking the path. We are following the Great Way.

WITH NO PREFERENCES

Preferences derive from our internal self-talk of "I like this" and "I do not like that." Our preferences support our customary self-identity. Only when we drop preferences, drop like and dislike, can we see the Great Way before us.

SURRENDER DESIRE AND AVERSION

In Buddhism we discuss three defilements. Defilements are core inclinations that drive the sense of self, making it appear real to us. The three defilements, which everyone has, are desire, aversion, and delusion.

Desire is a longing for things. We believe these things will make us feel safe and whole. Conversely, aversion is a dislike for things. We believe pushing bad things away from us will keep only good ones close. Finally, delusion is a misperception and misunderstanding of reality. We believe the customary self-identity is something real and solid.

By surrendering desire and aversion, we allow what is unfolding in our life to be here while viewing it as exactly right for this moment. We can be with the natural flow of reality.

CLARITY DAZZLES

By releasing desire and aversion, even temporarily, we can witness the natural quality of inner spaciousness. When concepts are few, we can see the dazzling clarity, the crispness, the precision, and the inherent perfection of our deeper true nature.

— *Do you see it, right here, right now?*

II.

ANY DISTINCTION

If we apply any concept or thought to our direct experience
with our true nature, we are stepping away from that direct
contact with inner truth and turning it into a conceptual
understanding. Our direct experience is immediately lost
whenever we form a concept to relate to or repeat that
experience. Any distinction we make, any concept we form
and apply, misses the mark of truth.

THE DISTANCE BETWEEN HEAVEN
AND EARTH

Heaven and earth are both right here in this moment of
eternal now. But when we confuse our conceptual understanding or memory of our true nature with our direct
experience of that nature, we separate heaven from earth.
When this happens, the smallest gap between our direct
experience and our conceptual understanding is akin to
the distance between heaven and earth.

In the Theravada map of the Buddha's path, "*nibbāna*" is the direct experience of Cessation in which all materiality and mentality cease. Cessation can happen when our consciousness (meaning our awareness plus our knowing) enters the unmanifest Absolute. *Nibbāna* is always awake. It is without any condition. It is not subject to birth and death. It has always existed and will always exist.

The Absolute contains both an unmanifest and a manifest function. The manifest function of the Absolute is where we encounter pure Presence, pure love, and pure awareness. These are the components that form all of physical reality. Everything we can perceive, witness, and experience is an expression of the Absolute in its manifest functioning.

In contrast, the unmanifest function is experienced as Absence and may be accompanied by a sense of peacefulness and deep stillness. It is without boundaries, a vastness, holding the pure potential from which everything arises and returns. As our consciousness enters the depths of this vast unmanifest Absence, any sense of a body or a distinct me disappears, concepts still, thoughts stop, and all perception of a discrete consciousness ceases. Even pure awareness, our direct awareness with no historical knowing, stops. The lights-out quality of Cessation is the experience of *nibbāna*.

We only know that Cessation has occurred after the lights come back on, after we return to consciousness and direct awareness resumes. Rather than feeling any kind of sluggishness upon reactivation after Cessation, we feel a bright clarity of awareness and precision of consciousness. We know something very special, extraordinary even, has just happened and is continuing. It is only as we reintegrate into our lives that we witness the changes from our experience of Cessation. We often find that previously troubling thoughts and behaviors and those of others do not cause the same reactions in us. Actions and words that would normally trigger our defensiveness do not ruffle our calm, accepting heart.

When we experience *nibbāna,* all materiality and mentality cease. Awakening of true Absolute reality blossoms concurrently in one particular location (in this particular consciousness as well as in awareness) as well as everywhere (all consciousness is impacted by that particular Awakening).

If the Awakening—called *kenshō* in Zen parlance—is short in duration, the normal sense of a me is temporarily displaced. The sense of a me later reappears. It is not as thoroughly believed, however.

Should the Awakening be sustained for weeks or months, more of our consciousness has awakened. The sense of a me may be displaced significantly, even to the point of our true nature replacing the sense of me as the foundation of identity.

ACQUITS FOR OR AGAINST

When we hold opinions for or against anything, we create a position in thought and concept. This conceptual position becomes an opinion we need to defend while convincing others of our rightness. Holding opinions for or against keeps us in the sense of self, in the me of opinion, evaluating and endlessly balancing right and wrong. It maintains a piece of our identity in that conclusion of for or against.

Nibbāna acquits notions of "for or against" as well as "right or wrong" in an undivided Oneness, a unity of love that embraces all and excludes nothing and no one. When we can rest in nonconceptual acceptance, we find we do not need to categorize our world as being either right or wrong, for or against.

— *Where is the truth in this very breath?*

III.

CLUTCH LIKES AND DISLIKES

When we hold tight to our likes and dislikes, we eliminate other possibilities. We fixate on the concept of only two options as answers to a particular issue: right or wrong. This position takes away all other possibilities for a different result.

Further, our customary self-identity is composed in part by the aggregation of our likes and dislikes. As we release and put down likes and dislikes, we become open to a variety of choices while untethering our sense of self from fixed opinions.

THE PRINCIPAL MIND DISEASE

In Buddhist practice, we notice that by holding fast to our particular likes and dislikes, we are continually recreating a sense of self that feels substantial or real. This deep-seated belief, this conviction, of the authenticity of the self is the principal mental hurdle to returning home to *nibbāna*.

In Awakening, we perceive that any sense of self is really an absence of self. The core of our beingness is actually a form of emptiness, an infinite spaciousness, a lack of substantiality. This absence of self does not hold opinions or positions. When deeply in absence of self, awareness finds itself in each new moment, with each fresh breath.

NOT CONSUMMATING TRUE NATURE

When we do not make contact regularly with our deeper true nature, we lose the perception that we intrinsically belong with all that manifests now, in this very moment.

Touching into our true nature has the felt-sense qualities both of being objective and unconditioned: objective in not reaffirming any sense of self; unconditioned in always being present right here now, rather than created or born.

We can make contact with our deeper true nature through different meditations and spiritual practices. The ancient Buddhist heart meditations are a way to directly touch and rest in the qualities of our true nature. (These meditations are presented in my book *Buddha's Heart*.)

AGITATES THE MIND

When we are not in contact with our true nature, we are unsettled, discontented, or ill at ease. We are agitated, trying to get from here to there, somewhere other than right here. We are seeking certain specific experiences to get away from who we take ourselves to be. The mental process of believing "I am here and I want to get or go there" stirs the mind and agitates our inherent peacefulness.

Resting in and as our true nature pacifies the choppy waves of self and our ceaseless efforts to fortify and maintain the customary sense of self. Resting in and as our true nature lets us relax deeply in the truth of who we are.

— *Where is your mind in this very moment?*

IV.

VAST, BOUNDLESS SPACE

The natural condition of our inner experience of awareness is space. Vast, boundless space. "Boundless" means we
cannot detect any edges or limits to the space. It is infinite.
When we are deeply in communion with this vast, inner
space, we feel profoundly at ease and connected to a deep
embedded truth of the universe: space is unlimited within.
All of reality arises from and returns to this infinite, alive
spaciousness. All spiritual or transcendental experiences are
available in this unending space.

PERFECT ABSENCE

Absence is the quality of having no abiding self—that
is, no longer perceiving reality through a conditioned
self-identity. For most people, our sense of self depends on
generating habitual thoughts, concepts, and closely held
opinions to reaffirm constantly who we take our selves to
be. Maintaining this separate self is psychologically con-
suming and deeply exhausting.

In the experience of Awakening, we deeply perceive
that we are the Absence quality of the Absolute and
particularly the experience of Cessation. I use the word

"Absence" over the customary word choice in Buddhism of "emptiness." "Emptiness" suggests nothing is there. "Absence" suggests something can be there, but is not in this particular moment. It is the possibility of an appearance from what is unmanifest into what is manifest. This is the potential of life.

PRESERVE PREFERENCES

When we maintain and preserve our preferences, we are confirming what we like and dislike as a foundation for our customary sense of self. The more invested we are in the sense of self, the further we have turned away from our true nature. By maintaining the polarity of like and dislike, we are maintaining a disharmonious attitude and perspective. We are stirring the deep, still waters of our true nature to create movement and activity. This activity of the mind then confirms the perceived reality of our sense of self and the movement of time from present to past to future.

CLOAK THE WISDOM EYE

The wisdom eye is an intuitive organ of perception that opens as we connect more deeply to the truth of who we are, to our true nature.

When we are deeply entrenched in our preferences, our polarities of opinion and belief, we turn away from our deepest true nature. In doing so we are implicitly rejecting our source, the truth of who we are. This turning away from our true nature to our customary sense of self cloaks the wisdom eye, denying us access to it.

The development of concentration meditation (such as breath awareness meditation, Zen *kōan* practice, and/or silent illumination meditation) or the Buddhist heart meditations called the *brahmavihāras* can open the wisdom eye.

— *Do you see?*

V.

REFRAIN FROM LIVING IN THE WORLD

This is not saying do not be in the world. It is saying do not live exclusively in the world. Ideally, we are resting in the inner spaciousness and unconditioned qualities of our true nature while conducting engaged lives in the world. There is an expression in Buddhism that fits here: "To live in the world but not of the world." This means we function as needed in our lives without taking the world as the deepest truth. Absence, indivisible Oneness, is the deepest truth and with it the source of all Cessation. And from Cessation arises creation.

REFRAIN FROM PURSUING ABSENCE

When we pursue an experience or realization, we are rejecting this moment and the fullness of its reality. We are looking to get from here to there. Our sense of self deludes us into making this anticipated move to obtain the freedom of living from and as our true nature. When we cease trying to get anywhere in our spiritual journey, the whole realization of truth is right at hand, here, now.

REPOSE IN HARMONIOUS LOVE

A unifying love provides the viscosity of the universe, the fuel for it. When we connect with this unconditioned, universal love, we feel its peaceful, harmonious balance. When we repose in this harmonious love, who we are becomes clear, and how to spontaneously and intuitively function from the heart of our true nature becomes clearer still.

POLARITIES GONE

As we recognize and rest in harmonious, unconditioned love, we stop identifying with our sense of self. We drop the polarities of right and wrong, here and there, you and me. We can simply be right here, without conceptually knowing what is happening. Clinging to thought and conceptual knowing provides an unnecessary veneer to what is unfolding. We rest in not knowing, which affords us direct, intuitive, embodied knowing based on direct experience.

— *Just this! Just this! Right here! Do you see?*

VI.

NOT TRAVERSING THE PATHWAY

When we are not actively traversing our spiritual path of unfolding, we wander aimlessly in the world. We feel we have lost our way, experiencing subtle and overt levels of confusion and uncertainty. These are the hallmarks of overly investing in our worldly views, rather than being on the Great Way.

JUDGMENTS BEWILDER

When we move through life stuck in our customary self-identity, believing it is the highest truth, we are besieged with judgments about all aspects of the life we witness and engage with. We see a growing list of likes and dislikes, concepts of understanding, and incessant habitual thoughts, all of which are generally in disharmony. The concepts arising may conflict with the thoughts or sense of self. The likes and dislikes may not match our customary self-identity. This disharmony leads to overlapping mental activity as we try to reconcile the divergent thoughts and concepts, resulting in our incessant confusion and bewilderment.

REGARD THE WORLDLY AS AUTHENTIC

When we act as if the usual everyday world is authentic and the source of all reality, we are confused, mistaken. By viewing our everyday world as the most authentic reality, we are rejecting the subtle yet fundamental truth that Cessation into Absence is the source of all creation. Rejecting truth and taking up what is inherently false leads to suffering, known as *dukkha* in Buddhism.

OBSCURE REALITY

By taking the everyday world as the source of all experience, we are actively obscuring the more profound levels of reality. The Absolute, particularly the Absence function and the experience of Cessation, is the source of all reality, both unconditioned and conditioned. When we awaken to the Absolute and our true nature as our true identity, we correct our view, perception, and understanding. Our Awakening reveals all of reality—seen and unseen—as intrinsically one, a unified field of loving aliveness.

— *What is the truth of this moment?*

VII.

REFUSE THE WORLDLY

Acceptance is an important function on the spiritual path. Whenever we feel a compulsion to rewind or fast forward any particular moment, we are not accepting what is right here, right now. We are not in touch with equanimity, a quality of our true nature. Conversely, we should not prefer or prioritize experiences of the Absolute.

We can conceptually prioritize that the transcendent, the territory of realization, and the experience of Awakening is better than the usual world we live in. Yet the everyday world is also a manifestation of the Absolute, of Absence. When we refuse the everyday world, we are also rejecting the source of that world: the Absolute. It is a mistake to view the everyday world and all it contains as less than or in any way different from the Absolute.

VEIL THE ABSOLUTE

By refusing the world in preference for the experiences, realizations, and Awakenings of the Absolute, we concurrently obscure the Absolute. In rejecting any aspect of reality, we reject all aspects of reality. In refusing the worldly as being different than the Absolute, we veil the Absolute.

PROPAGATE THOUGHT AND CONCEPT

When we actively engage in thought and the application of concepts in viewing ourselves or the world, we prioritize mentality over direct knowing. We are layering concepts over the clear, vast, spacious realm of awareness. This propagation of thoughts and concepts limits us from the path of spiritual development and the unfolding of Awakening.

ELUDE TRUTH

When we overinvest meaning in our thoughts and concepts, we are not being directly with undiluted, pure truth. We are rejecting one way the Absolute appears in the world as the world: Absence in form. By prioritizing thought and concept over direct embodied knowing, we are left confused and actively eluding truth.

— *What are you seeing in this moment?*

VIII.

UNBIND THOUGHT AND CONCEPT

As we rely more upon inner intuitive knowing, seeing, hearing, tasting, and touching, we unbind thought and concept from defining and maintaining the placement of reality. We relax our allegiance to thought and concept; we withdraw from them. We may witness firsthand that the inner knowing of Absence holds objective truths that are unconditioned, that are not subject to birth or death. These are everlasting qualities of true nature always fully available in our consciousness.

ROAM OPENLY

When we roam openly, we traverse the length and breadth of our inner spaciousness, of our consciousness, from this world to other universes, including the source of the Absolute. When we are not invested in maintaining a particular self, we are home everywhere. We can then rest in knowing the wholeness of perfection of manifested reality, what actually is here.

INHABIT THE SOURCE

When we inhabit the source, we become a vessel, a conduit, through which the Absolute flows, witnessing itself as the source and manifestation of all reality. Rest in the truth that you are fully Absence and Presence.

KNOW ALL MEANING

When Absence, true nature, and the Absolute are the sources we check in with to confirm our identity, we understand everything in proper relationship. There is nothing added or subtracted in reality. When we abide continuously in pure love and Presence, see the world in all its divergent parts as being expressions of seamless love coupled with Presence, we know all meaning.

— *Everything is right here, right now. Do you see it?*

IX.

AWAKENING DAWNS

When our consciousness wakes to the present reality of our true nature, we know "this is me/I am this" always and without qualification, and Awakening recognizes itself. True nature as our core abides without insisting, waiting to be experientially witnessed. When we witness it or rather when true nature witnesses itself, Awakening dawns.

ECLIPSE FORM AND ABSENCE

In sustained deeper Awakening experiences, we drop everything because we are resting in the embodied knowing, the unrestricted perception of the infinite Oneness of all reality. We drop all concepts and all realities built upon the foundation of fabricated, conditioned thought. Even the conceptual positions of form and Absence are eclipsed. In reality, there is no form or Absence. When we dwell in no form and absence of form, then we truly know form and Absence by direct contact rather than through conceptual frameworks, affording us direct knowing.

NO BEGINNING, NO END

When we hold the concepts of a beginning and an end, we commit to the passage of time from past to present to future. But all time is an unconditioned present moment. The unending present moment. It is free from birth and death. It has always existed and always will exist. No beginning or end means right here, right now, nothing added or deducted. When we are one with Cessation—with Absence and simultaneously Presence—we see there is nowhere to go and no one to go there. We have already arrived.

SEVER EVERY OPINION

We must voluntarily release any and every opinion about the world, even the world of Awakening. We must sever ourselves from opinions about Cessation, the unmanifest, the manifest, pure love, pure Presence, pure awareness, and the lack of these. All are points of view. Reality always is, right here and right now.

— *Where are you looking?*

X.

ABIDING IN ABSENCE

Absence is a core quality of Cessation and the unmanifest functioning of the Absolute. It is a core quality of each being in creation. When we are not deluded by appearances, we rest in and as Absence, in and as the boundless potential of vast spaciousness.

CONCEIT HUMBLES

One of the last opinions to fall away is conceit. It is not conceit in worldly abilities but rather in the experience of realization itself. A mind harboring conceit because of realization is not a mind resting in and functioning from realization itself. This clinging to experience reveals that despite deep realization, investigation of personal conceptual convictions and beliefs remains. This is the ceaselessness of the spiritual path. There is no end to realizations and no end to unconscious personal material needing to be engaged, excised, and liberated.

Realization does not make us special. It makes us profoundly ordinary. We become a conduit for our true nature, for truth to spontaneously, joyfully, authentically express itself as it wishes and as needed. We are the servants of truth, which is the Absolute in its manifest and unmanifest functions.

RESIDING IN WISDOM

"Wisdom" means to see clearly and take action that is appropriate, attuned precisely to what is needed in each new moment. Wisdom is not discerned by concept or thought. There is no self to get anything, to go anywhere, or to be anyone in particular. Then we can be unique, special, and express true nature's wisdom with a natural, authentic humility.

QUIET CONFIDENCE

When concepts and thoughts are stilled, profound quiet serenity pervades our consciousness. Seeing there is no me or you, no here or there, no time other than the endless now, our confidence is expressed as a lack of hesitation, of questioning, and of doubt. Truth knows itself. From intimately knowing itself, truth can be perfectly attuned in each moment.

— Where is your seat in this moment?

CEASELESS FREEDOM

Having no allegiance to any thought, belief, concept, experience, or timeframe affords us the freedom to be here right now, endlessly. Whether in form or abiding as formless reality, our true nature is free, unencumbered, unrestrained in a spontaneous, ceaseless flow.

ABIDING IN CLARITY

With no doubts, our consciousness radiates clarity. When there is nowhere to go, no one to go there, and nothing to do when arriving or leaving, we abide right here in the now.

UNMANIFEST AND MANIFEST ABSOLUTE

A deep realization recognizes both functions of the Absolute, the manifest and unmanifest, as nothing but Absence. The unmanifest is the foundation of the manifest. Without the unmanifest—the raw power of deep Absence—there cannot be manifestation through Presence and love, and the resulting appearance of form. The unmanifest is the power that, combined with qualities of the manifest—pure Presence and pure love—creates all of life as we witness it in each breath moment.

IMMACULATE NON-DOING

Usually, we take action because our thoughts and concepts support a compulsive need to be seen, mirrored, and valued. When we have no sense of self, no core egoistic deficiency, no sense of worthlessness abiding in us, we lack a compulsive driver of our doing and behavior. Instead, we just are. We just are here. We just are now. From this pristine clarity, non-doing—wise and intuitive action—happens, appearing on the canvas of reality.

— *Where are you right now?*

XII

MOVE FREELY

Stillness is the same as movement in the world of Absence and Presence. When movement and stillness are the same, there is complete freedom. Moving or not moving are concepts, not the functioning of the Absolute. We see the Great Way as traversing a mighty mountain yet simultaneously not going anywhere but here.

ETERNAL NOW

Time is just a way to explain the movement of the Absolute. The past and the future are purely concepts, because the Absolute moves yet does not depart from here. With no past and no future, we witness abiding in the eternal present moment, the eternal now. Right now, the Buddha is preaching the dharma. Right now, our great-grandchildren are playing together at a neighborhood park.

NO LOCUS OF AWARENESS

Generally, when we make an observation of inner or outer reality we have a vantage point, a locus of perspective. This is subjective seeing. As our realization of true nature deepens, the markers of self fall away, and we lose the locus of me or mine. As the immersion in and as Oneness deepens and stabilizes, our perspective then shifts from subjective to objective, which has no locus of perspective or awareness. We know that all of reality exists as and in a unified field of Oneness.

SUCHNESS UNFOLDS

Suchness is the reality when all concepts and thoughts have fallen away in importance. When we are deeply resting in the Absence quality of the unmanifest and the pure Presence quality of the manifest, suchness is here. When everything falls away and we abide in beingness, suchness is present. Whenever we perceive suchness, it is unfolding in its potency and Presence. The heart no longer braces against reality. Everything is exactly right.

— *Where are you in this moment?*

XIII.

KALĀPA UNIVERSE

In Buddhism, a *kalāpa* is a subatomic particle. It contains all the qualities and attributes of the universe. Scientists confirm the universe and all forms of reality are composed entirely of *kalāpas*. Physical reality—called materiality in Buddhism—is really just *kalāpas* joined together.

DISSOLVING BOUNDARIES

When our consciousness and awareness journey to the edges of the inner universe, we find no edge, no end, no limit. In each direction no endpoint exists. We just find pulsating, alive vastness without beginning or end. We feel the boundarylessness as the most profound freedom of pure, still contentment, a confirmation there is no beginning or end. We have nothing to fear or worry about. We have thorough trust in all that is unfolding, in each and every moment.

UNIVERSE KALĀPA

In the reality of the Absolute each part contains the whole. A speck of dust contains all universes. Each vibrating, pulsating *kalāpa* contains the whole, all of reality, as it abides in and functions as Absence and Presence.

OPENLY UNCONDITIONED

When we start our journey to Awakening, we feel safe in what is conditioned. We know if it can be born and die, it is precious. As our allegiance to ingrained concept and thought lessens and eventually falls away, we develop greater comfort in being Absence, having Absence flow and function as us. We see that nothing is truly conditioned; everything is Absence functioning as a flow of pure love, pure Presence, and pure awareness. Our sense of being safe and free shifts to reside openly in unconditioned Absence. In unconditioned Absence we peacefully abide in the knowing experience that the Universe is mysterious, loving, and far outside any belief in an us or a me.

— *Where do you reside?*

XIV.

BEING IS NON-BEING

By penetrating concept and thought, the Absolute arises as our true nature. All being, all Presence is right here, abiding in and as the world of form. The world of being—all we are, all we witness, all our functioning in the everyday world—is nothing but the activity of Absence and Presence, nothing but non-being.

ABSENCE

No qualities, no location, even no name. Abiding in Absence is pure freedom. There are no compulsions, no demands, no habits of mind. With no here or there, no now or later, there is no movement or distance and also no limitation of movement and distance. With direct knowing we understand without explanation.

NON-BEING IS BEING

Absence moves from its unmanifest function of non-being to its manifest functioning of being. Every form we can witness is the full and loving expression of Absence powering Presence and love into manifesting all realities. Form appears, abides, and disappears.

MANIFESTATION

All creation arises from the pure love, profound Presence and pristine awareness, of the manifest function of the Absolute. This pure love is a germinating life force, propelling that seed to sprout into life after receiving enough soil, water, and sun. From Absence, unmanifest Absence comes into being as manifest Presence through a germination, of creation and manifestation.

— *What are you made of?*

XV.

DIAMONDLIKE CLARITY

This refers to our experience of multifaceted knowing. The wisdom eye can see reality directly with a diamond-like clarity. At times we can perceive not only what is in awareness but also other subtle layers of reality. For example, if we were to enter the field of awareness, our perception might be of how invested we are in our sense of self. In addition, we could perceive how open or closed our heart is to love. We might also glimpse into our karmic stream based upon deep contact in this moment.

VISION PENETRATES

The vision of knowing can penetrate the structure of our sense of self. We can witness what is apparent on the surface or a relative layer but also what lies in deeper levels of reality where the infinite Absolute is directly experienced. The open wisdom eye can have deep intuitive knowing about personal workings. But it also at times can penetrate the surface waves and witness the ocean of love, of Oneness, beneath the surface of life.

ABSENCE IS FORM

A certain depth of consciousness can be experientially known. That level is where all form, all material reality, is witnessed simultaneously as Absence appearing in physical reality. Absence needs form to recognize itself in an Awakening experience and to point us back through reflective practices and capacities to knowing the source, the fabric of all reality, as Absence. Absence needs the manifest for each of us to realize, awaken to, and embody Absence and Presence.

FORM IS ABSENCE

All of physical reality has love and Presence as its core function and flow. When physical reality is perceived and known to have Absence at its functioning core, we understand form is Absence and Absence is form, always in this interplay of Absence and physicality. It is not that Absence becomes form or form returns to Absence. They are each fully the other, always.

— *What is the felt sense of Absence is form*
   and form is Absence?

XVI.

AWAKE

Awakening experiences open our consciousness to the multilayered reality of life. We can be aware simultaneously of a physical level, Absence and Presence qualities, and psychological structures. In other words, the personality can be perceived while also directly experiencing the depth of Absence and the functioning of Presence and love. This is awakeness.

WHO IS HOLY OR WISE

Should we wish to be seen by others as holy or wise, it usually indicates we are neither. It is the subtlety of conceit of the spiritual experience that is operating. After the sense of self, the me, is thoroughly seen through to its core conviction of deficiency and that deficiency is resolved, the self-identity drops and does not return. The simple functioning of love replaces the clinging and grasping motivations of the customary self-identity. How can the core of Absence have any desire, even any wish, to be seen as holy or wise? When we truly know through direct experience what we genuinely are, we know simultaneously what everyone is. Everything is unfolding in a unified field of love and Presence.

UNINHIBITED TRUST

When we see the Absolute abiding as the source and core of all reality, we perceive and know the universe is intrinsically benevolent and well-intentioned toward all. We have a thorough, uninhibited trust that all will be well and love will always heal hatred.

HEARTFUL MODESTY

As the Absolute functions as a particular person or other being, it is functioning as love and Presence. Love is at the cellular core of all intention and action. The Absolute is contacting Absence and Presence in every single interchange, moment by moment. We have no urge to control or direct any aspect of reality because of our arising trust in the love quality of the Absolute. We also recognize that we never have all the information to fully understand the subtlety of the Absolute's functioning. Both this core love and acknowledgement of the Absolute's subtlety opens a natural, authentic humility in us, a heartful modesty.

— *Do you claim your spiritual experiences?*

XVII.

HEAVENLY CONTENTMENT

When we know with every fiber of our being that love and Presence are the function of the Absolute appearing in the everyday world, reality opens our awareness to the peace that surpasses understanding. This peace is the contentment, the uncontracted satisfaction, of the heavens operating as our everyday world. What more can we ever need? Everything necessary is always right here, resting here, offering itself with breathtaking generosity and thorough abundance without insistence.

WITHOUT PAST OR FUTURE

With no self-identity functioning, we give no weight to the concepts of past or future. There is just this particular moment, always. Landing here affords us a freedom from regret of the past and from compulsive planning to ensure a particular future. This does not mean we can avoid the work of healing from past trauma and of reconciling our past with its landmines of guilt and shame. It does mean we do what is obvious and wholehearted in this moment, seeking always to be true to the purity and clarity of the Absolute.

WITHOUT HERE OR THERE

All time and all locations are always present, right here and right now. When the concepts of time and distance drop, there is only an eternal now and an eternal here. When awareness is everywhere, how do we divide everywhere into a here or a there?

TRUST IN AWAKENING

Awakening challenges our firm conviction in our sense of self and our being in a particular point in time as delusion. Our commitment to the customary self-identity omits the truth of the Absolute: love and Presence are the creative, generative forces of all reality. Only through the process of Awakening can we know that the self, as we hold it, is all Absence and Presence of the Absolute. And Absence and Presence are both propelled by pure love.

As Awakening then deepens through penetration of increasingly subtle levels of reality, the roots and defenses of our customary self-identity weaken and fall away. All our action and all we witness is realized as an expression, a function, of love. This pure love generates wholesome trust in the benevolence of the Absolute. We then know and trust that love is always returning to itself as each and every form, always in this very moment, right here. Experiencing further levels of reality, we experience deeper and deeper trust in the reality of Awakening.

— *Do you trust in Awakening?*

Glossary

Absence: Absence is a synonym for emptiness in Buddhism. It is a quality of reality where there is nothing apparent to ordinary perception yet something substantial and significant is present and perceived intuitively, directly through experiential contact.

absence of self: The experience of the customary self-identity being increasingly transparent and difficult to locate within.

Absolute: The source of all life animation, all form, and formless reality.

awareness: Perception, with or without consciousness, of internal and external events unfolding.

beingness: Unconditioned Presence.

brahmavihāras: Ancient Buddhist heart meditations that open our awareness to unconditioned qualities of our true nature such as equanimity (*upekkha*), empathetic joy (*mudita*), compassion (*karuna*), unconditioned love (*metta*), and innate goodness, to name a few.

breath awareness meditation: Breath awareness meditation (*anapanasati*). Typically, the first meditation given to new students by the Buddha. This practice concentrates and purifies the mind through turning away from the habituated thinking and routine concepts. This practice can lead to the deepest level of meditative concentration called *jhāna*. (Please see my book *Practicing the Jhānas* for details on this practice.)

Cessation: The experience of complete merging into Absence, the peace, the pure stillness of the unmanifest Absolute. All mentality and materiality ceases, including consciousness and awareness.

Ch'an: The Chinese Buddhist tradition of using *kōan* and silent illumination meditation to open and directly experience Cessation and likely an Awakening experience.

concentration meditation: A collection of meditations in which the meditator stays with one meditative object to the exclusion of all other sense data or experience.

consciousness: Awareness coupled with ordinary and intuitive knowing.

dharma: Teaching or universal law. Also known as *dhamma*.

***dukkha*:** The first noble truth of Buddhism that human life contains dissatisfactoriness/suffering.

eternal now: The true measure of time. The past and future are concepts only. The present moment is the only unit of time and experience.

felt sense: Intuitive perception of what is not visually apparent.

***kalāpas*:** Subatomic particles of conditioned reality.

***kenshō*:** Seeing into one's true nature; from the Zen tradition's map of Awakening.

***nibbāna*:** An experience of Cessation in which all materiality and mentality cease. Also known as *nirvāṇa*.

Oneness: The function of the Absolute and all universes is a unified, indivisible unity.

path of no path: A path of no path means an inner journey where ordinary doing is insufficient. It is only by being, rather than doing, that we journey on this path. The path of no path is nonconceptual and directly, immediately known through experience.

Presence: Experiential contact with the beingness quality of this present moment.

realm: A location of reality that is perceived to be outside ordinary reality.

self-identity: The psychological patterns of mind and behavior that define who we are to ourselves; self-concept; self-recognition.

silent illumination meditation: The Chinese Ch'an Buddhist meditation of being awareness to unify 1) body/mind, 2) inside/outside, and 3) the vastness of inner spaciousness without conceptual boundaries.

suchness: The experience of Presence and Absence combined functioning of the Absolute in this very location and time.

Theravada Buddhism: The tradition of Buddhism maintaining the traditional meditative practices of the Buddha.

true nature: The true, core foundation of unconditioned reality. The source of all universes, the Absolute, as it abides in our individual consciousness.

wisdom eye: The intuitive, psychic mode of perception that can open to support deep inner seeing and support inner knowing.

Zen Buddhism: The Buddhist tradition that evolved from Chinese Ch'an Buddhism. Awakening is the primary objective.

Zen *kōan* practice: The awakening stories from ancient Ch'an or Zen students and masters that modern students reflect upon to reveal the intuitive answer to the paradox in the *kōan*. A system organized to support students' awakening/*kenshō* experiences.

About the Author

STEPHEN DOETSU SNYDER began practicing daily meditation in 1976. Since then, he has studied Buddhism extensively— investigating and engaging in Zen, Tibetan, Theravada, and Western non-dual traditions. He was authorized to teach in the Theravada Buddhist tradition in 2007 and the Zen Buddhist schools of Soto and Rinzai in 2022.

Stephen's resonant and warmhearted teaching style engages students around the globe through in-person and online retreats, as well as one-on-one coaching. He encourages students to turn toward their true nature and, with realization of their true nature, embody their true identity. Stephen is the author of three books, including *Demystifying Awakening* and *Buddha's Heart*. He also co-authored *Practicing the Jhānas*. For more information, please visit awakeningdharma.org.

Did you Benefit from Trust in Awakening?

SHARE YOUR PRAISE

Did this book offer new insights into Buddhist teachings that are benefiting your daily life or interactions? If so, a review shared through your favorite online retailer would be warmly welcomed. A few minutes of your time could help others find this book and benefit as you have.

PLACE A BULK ORDER

Would you like to share this book with a group or a class? Please be in touch! We can offer bulk discounts for orders of ten or more copies to most locations. Please write to buddhasheartpress @gmail.com.

KEEP IN TOUCH

For more about Stephen's books, workshops, and other offerings, please visit awakeningdharma.org.

Also by Stephen Snyder

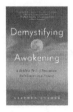

Demystifying Awakening: A Buddhist Path of Realization, Embodiment, and Freedom
HARDCOVER · 978-1-7347810-6-9 · $24.95
E-BOOK · 978-1-7347810-5-2 · $9.95
PUBLISHED MARCH 2022

A practice path in the process of Awakening—in this lifetime. *Demystifying Awakening* clearly explains experiences of Awakening, highlighting the natural resistances and how to work with them; outlines steps for developing a wholesome livelihood: the natural embodiment of realization; and offers extensive meditations and practices that support each step on the path.

Buddha's Heart: Meditation Practice for Developing Well-Being, Love, and Empathy
PAPERBACK · 978-1-7347810-2-1 · $16.95
E-BOOK · 978-1-7347810-3-8 · $9.95
PUBLISHED NOVEMBER 2020

An original and clear path to the powerful *brahmavihāras*—ancient Buddhist heart practices. These practices offer rich, soothing support for the soul and a portal to spiritual awakening and deepening self-realization. *Buddha's Heart* teaches what seems counterintuitive but is undeniably true: the more we open our hearts, the more resilient and flexible we are. And the more authentically vulnerable we are, the safer and more protected we become.

Stress Reduction for Lawyers, Law Students,
and Legal Professionals: Learning to Relax

PAPERBACK · 978-1-7347810-0-7 · $14.95

E-BOOK · 978-1-7347810-1-4 · $9.95

PUBLISHED SEPTEMBER 2020

A practical guide for a more relaxed and enjoyable legal career—authored by a retired lawyer and senior meditation teacher. This book offers straightforward techniques to identify the events that cause stress in your work, apply practices that support deep relaxation, and develop greater satisfaction in your work and personal life.

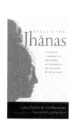

Practicing the Jhānas: Traditional
Concentration Meditation as Presented
by the Venerable Pa Auk Sayadaw

PAPERBACK · 978-1-59030-733-5 · $22.95

E-BOOK · 978-0-8348-2282-5 · $17.99

PUBLISHED DECEMBER 2009

COAUTHORED WITH TINA RASMUSSEN

A clear and in-depth presentation of the traditional Theravada concentration meditation known as *jhāna* practice, developed from practicing *jhāna* meditation in retreat under the guidance of one of the great living meditation masters, the Venerable Pa Auk Sayadaw.

Made in United States
Troutdale, OR
10/23/2023

13955504R00072